THE LEGEND OF BIGFOOT

by Thomas Kingsley Troupe   illustrated by Brian Caleb Dumm

PICTURE WINDOW BOOKS

a capstone imprint

Thanks to our advisers for their expertise, research, and advice:

Elizabeth Tucker, Professor of English
Binghamton University
Binghamton, New York

Terry Flaherty, PhD, Professor of English
Minnesota State University, Mankato

Editor: Jennifer Besel
Designer: Nathan Gassman
Production Specialist: Jane Klenk
The illustrations in this book were created digitally.

Picture Window Books
151 Good Counsel Drive
P.O. Box 669
Mankato, MN 56002-0669
877-845-8392
www.capstonepub.com

All books published by Picture Window Books
are manufactured with paper containing at least
10 percent post-consumer waste.

Library of Congress Cataloging-in-Publication Data
Troupe, Thomas Kingsley.
The legend of Bigfoot / by Thomas Kingsley Troupe ; illustrated by
Brian Caleb Dumm.
p. cm.—(Legend has it)
Includes bibliographical references and index.
Summary: "Describes the legend of Bigfoot, including how it started and what the
legend says about the monster"—Provided by publisher.
ISBN 978-1-4048-6032-2 (lib. bdg.)
1. Sasquatch—Juvenile literature. I. Title. II. Series.
QL89.2.S2T76 2011
001.944—dc22   2009050173

Printed in the United States of America in North Mankato, Minnesota.
042011   006171R

TABLE of CONTENTS

BIGFOOT BEGINNINGS

Heavy steps pound the forest floor. Branches snap, and a loud roar echoes through the hills.

A mighty bigfoot approaches!

Stories about giant apelike men started in the late 1700s. They say monsters called bigfoots stomp through the forests of North America.

Are bigfoots real? No one knows for sure. In 1901, Mike King swore he saw a hairy man-beast by a river. Frightened, the creature roared and ran away.

Did King see a bigfoot?

Over time, more sightings were reported.
In 1957, Albert Ostman claimed he had been
kidnapped by bigfoots. Ostman was
camping. He said he was scooped up in his
sleeping bag. Something big carried him to a
group of hairy creatures. Ostman **escaped
after six days.**

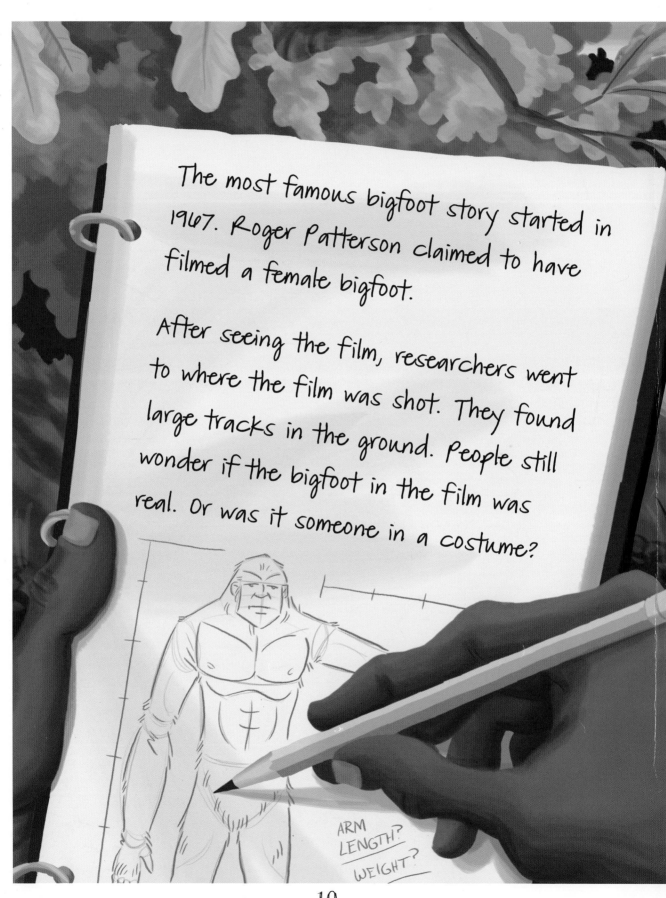

The most famous bigfoot story started in 1967. Roger Patterson claimed to have filmed a female bigfoot.

After seeing the film, researchers went to where the film was shot. They found large tracks in the ground. People still wonder if the bigfoot in the film was real. Or was it someone in a costume?

ARM LENGTH?

WEIGHT?

BIG, HAIRY, and SCARY

Some people believe that up to 6,000 bigfoots live in North America. They think bigfoots live where humans cannot find them. Wooded hills would be great places for them to live.

That is, if they are real.

TOP 10 PLACES TO SPOT A BIGFOOT

1. **Washington, USA (486 sightings)**
2. **California, USA (416 sightings)**
3. **Oregon, USA (223 sightings)**
4. **Ohio, USA (205 sightings)**
5. **Texas, USA (177 sightings)**
6. **Florida, USA (171 sightings)**
7. **Michigan, USA (117 sightings)**
8. **British Columbia, Canada (115 sightings)**
9. **Illinois, USA (109 sightings)**
10. **Colorado, USA (105 sightings)**

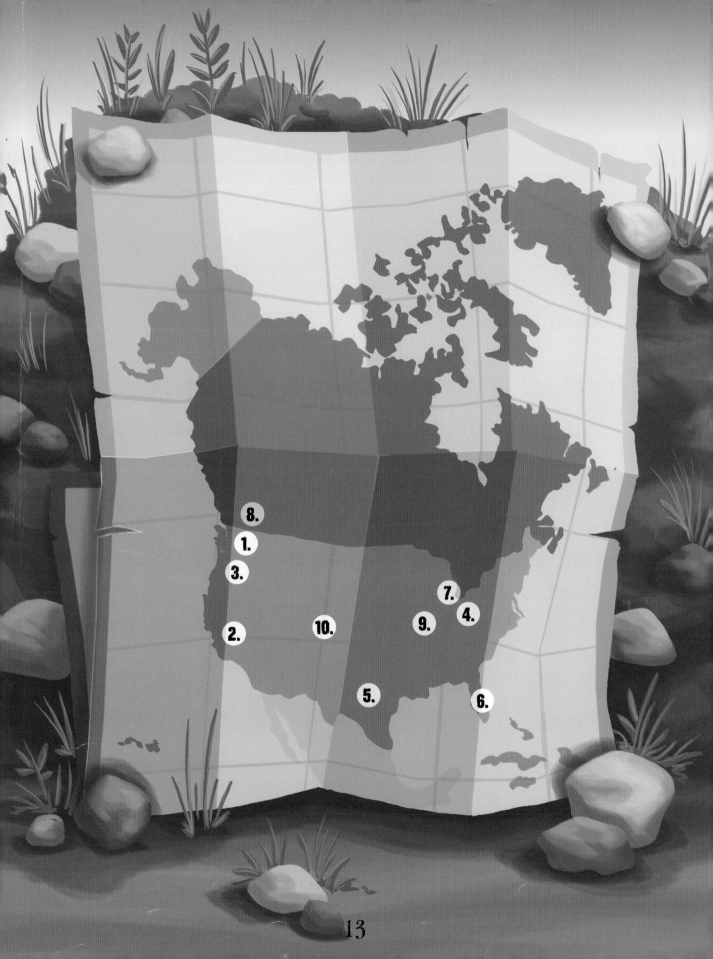

Legend says that a bigfoot stands 7 to 10 feet (213 to 305 centimeters) tall. An adult bigfoot weighs up to 900 pounds (408 kilograms).

10 ft
8
6
4
2

The bigfoot name comes, of course, from the creatures' giant feet. Researchers claim to have found a footprint that was 27 inches (69 centimeters) long!

Some people claim to have found bigfoot prints that have two toes. Other prints have five or six toes.

Bigfoots are covered in **thick hair.** They have **long arms** that hang to their knees. Beneath their hair, they are said to have **strong muscles** that can uproot trees and fling boulders.

Legend has it that bigfoots stink!

Some people claim that the monsters smell like sweat, poop, and rotten meat.

WHAT ARE BIGFOOTS?

No one knows without a doubt if bigfoots exist.
But if they do, some people have ideas about
what they really are.

One idea is that bigfoots are an early form of
human. Stories say bigfoots walk like humans.

Others believe bigfoots are apes. Their long arms are a lot like those of apes. Bigfoots, however, are much taller than gorillas.

Are bigfoots something else? Some believe bigfoots are a new kind of animal. Bigfoots could be an animal no one has discovered!

Whatever it is, a creature the size of a bigfoot would have a large appetite. Some think bigfoots eat both plants and animals.

BIGFOOTS
around the WORLD

Many other places have bigfoot stories. In Australia, many believe in a creature known as the **yowie.**

Like bigfoots, the yowie is thought to live in the woods and hills. It is hairy and walks like a human.

In Canada, bigfoots are called **Sasquatch.**
Many people believe Canada's Sasquatch and
the United States' bigfoot are the same creature.

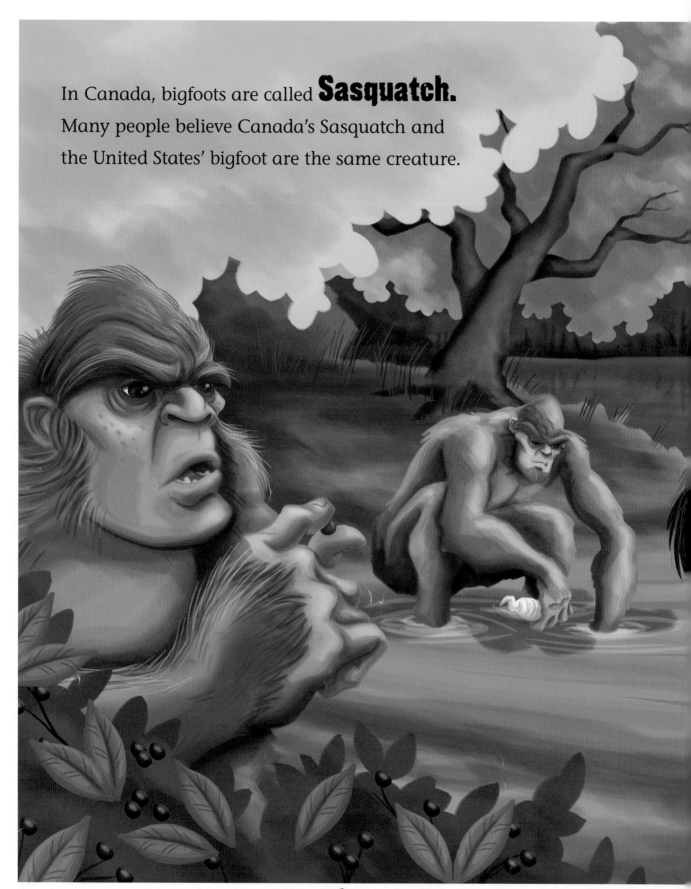

In Nepal and Tibet, legendary creatures called the

yeti live in the Himalaya Mountains. According to stories, the yeti enjoy the cold and snow. These creatures are sometimes called abominable snowmen.

Stories about bigfoots excite people around the world. But no one knows if the stories are true. Could those giant footprints be from **huge, hairy monsters?**

What do you think?

GLOSSARY

appetite—hunger for food

claim—to say something is true

doubt—uncertainty

exist—to live or to be real

kidnap—to capture a person and keep him or her as a prisoner

legend—a story handed down from earlier times that could seem believable

track—a mark left behind by a moving animal or person

READ MORE

DeMolay, Jack. *Bigfoot: A North American Legend.* Jr. Graphic Mysteries. New York: PowerKids Press, 2007.

McCormick, Lisa Wade. *Bigfoot: The Unsolved Mystery.* Mysteries of Science. Mankato, Minn.: Capstone Press, 2009.

Worth, Bonnie. *Looking for Bigfoot.* Step into Reading. New York: Random House, 2010.

INTERNET SITES

FactHound offers a safe, fun way to find Internet sites related to this book. All of the sites on FactHound have been researched by our staff.

Here's all you do:

Visit *www.facthound.com*

FactHound will fetch the best sites for you!

INDEX

LEGEND HAS IT
OTHER TITLES

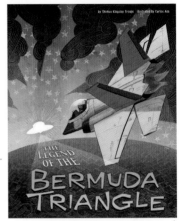

The Legend of the Bermuda Triangle

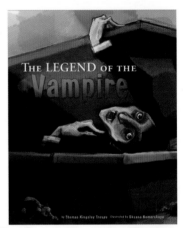

The Legend of the Vampire

The Legend of the Werewolf